What's Living Inside Your Body?

Andrew Solway

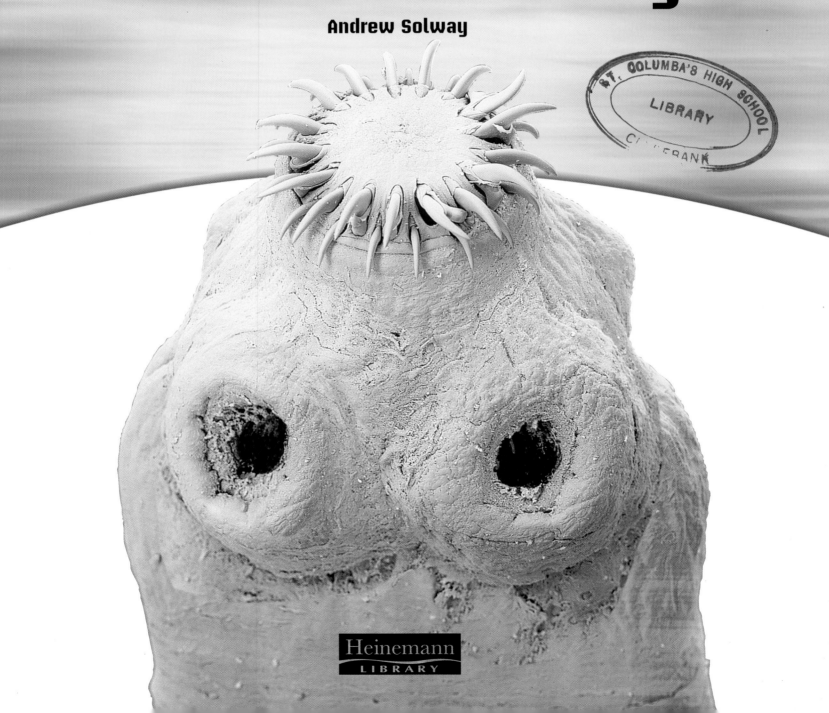

Heinemann
LIBRARY

www.heinemann.co.uk/library
Visit our website to find out more information about **Heinemann Library** books.

To order:
☎ Phone 44 (0) 1865 888066
🖹 Send a fax to 44 (0) 1865 314091
💻 Visit the Heinemann Bookshop at www.heinemann.co.uk/library to browse our catalogue and order online.

First published in Great Britain by
Heinemann Library, Halley Court,
Jordan Hill, Oxford OX2 8EJ, part of
Harcourt Education.
Heinemann is a registered trademark of
Harcourt Education Ltd.

© Harcourt Education Ltd 2004
The moral right of the proprietor has been
asserted.

Editorial: Nancy Dickmann and Tanvi Rai
Design: David Poole and Paul Myerscough
Illustrations: Geoff Ward
Picture Research: Rebecca Sodergren
Production: Séverine Ribierre

Originated by Dot Gradations
Printed and bound in China by South China
Printing Company

The paper used to print this book comes
from sustainable resources.

ISBN 0 431 189625
08 07 06 05 04
10 9 8 7 6 5 4 3 2 1

**British Library Cataloguing in
Publication Data**
Solway, Andrew
Hidden Life: What's Living Inside Your Body?
  616'.01
A full catalogue record for this book is
available from the British Library.

Acknowledgements
The publishers would like to thank the
following for permission to reproduce
photographs:

Trevor Clifford p. **22L**; Science Photo Library
pp. **10r**, **11**, **20**; Science Photo Library
p. **26b** (Michael Abbey), p. **16** (Juergen
Berger, Max Planck Institute), p. **6b** (Dr
Tony Brain), p. **8** (BSIP, Vero/Carlo), p. **21t**
(CAMR/Barry Dowsett), p. **24** (Jack K. Clark)
pp. **6t**, **9b**, **15** (CNRI), pp. **14**, **17**, **23**, **26t**,
27t, **27b** (Eye of Science), p. **4** (Simon
Fraser), p. **25** (Dr Gary Gaugler), pp. **12**, **19**
(Dr P. Marazzi), p. **9t** (Prof. P. Motta),
p. **18b**, (Susumu Nishinaga), pp. **16t**, **17t**,
18t (Alfred Pasieka), p. **5** (R. Maisonneuve,
Publiphoto Diffusion), p. **21b** (Chris Priest
and Mark Clarke), p. **13** (David Scharf), pp.
10L, **22r** (Dr Linda Stannard, UCT), p. **7**
(Volker Steger).

Cover photograph of a hookworm,
reproduced with permission of Science
Photo Library/David Scharf.

Every effort has been made to contact
copyright holders of any material
reproduced in this book. Any omissions will
be rectified in subsequent printings if notice
is given to the publishers.

The paper used to print this book comes
from sustainable resources.

Contents

Any words appearing in the text in bold, **like this,** are explained in the Glossary.

Many of the photos in this book were taken using a microscope. In the captions you may see a number that tells you how much they have been enlarged. For example, a photo marked '(x200)' is about 200 times bigger than in real life.

Taking a closer look

We all know that germs can cause disease if they get inside our bodies. We wash our hands before we eat so that we don't get germs on our food, and we clean cuts and grazes carefully to stop them getting infected with germs. 'Germs' are **microbes** – tiny living things too small to see without a microscope.

Microbes can cause disease, but even if you are not ill there are microbes inside your body – lots of them! There are more microbes living inside you than there are humans on the planet. Most cause no harm, and some are positively helpful. Nearly all these microbes live in your nose, mouth and gut, but sometimes they get into the blood or other parts of the body, and make you ill.

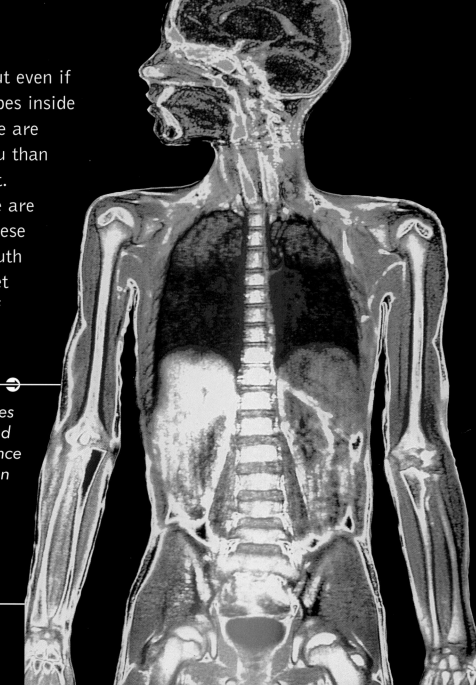

Modern techniques such as X-rays and magnetic resonance imaging (MRI) can look inside the body, but these techniques don't show the hidden life inside us.

Unwelcome visitors

We can also get bigger animals living inside us – **parasites** such as **tapeworms** and **hookworms**. However, these parasites do not commonly infect humans in **developed countries**. The idea of having worms living inside you is pretty horrible, but you can actually have some types of worm inside you without getting ill.

Smaller residents

Microbes are much more common in the body than larger creatures. Most of the microbes in our bodies are **bacteria**. Different kinds of bacteria can be as different from each other as we are from insects. For some kinds of bacteria our gut is their home, and they live there happily without doing us harm. But if other types get inside us, they can cause disease. Luckily our bodies have many defence systems against disease-causing microbes.

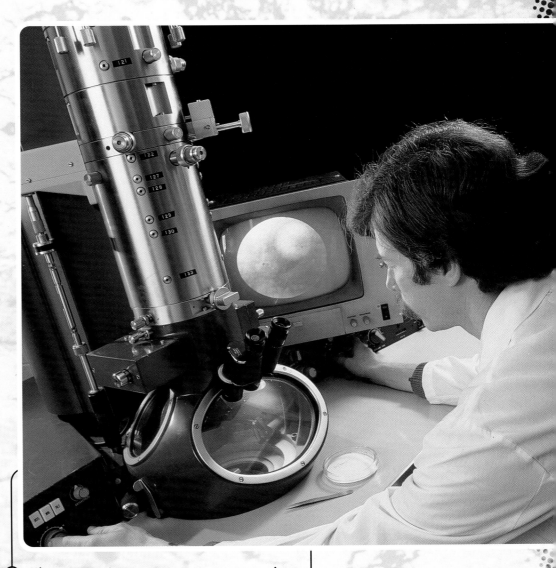

Electron microscopes are expensive and difficult to use, but they can magnify objects much more than a light microscope can.

MICROSCOPES

We know so much about the hidden life all around us because scientists have studied these things using microscopes. The type of microscope you may have used yourself at home or at school (a light microscope) can magnify object up to about 1800 times. But to look at really tiny things such as bacteria, scientists use powerful **electron microscopes**, which can magnify objects half a million times.

Microbes in the mouth

Every time you eat or put anything into your mouth, you put **microbes** in there too. You begin doing this from the first time you feed or suck your thumb as a baby. Most of the microbes that get into the mouth die, but some survive.

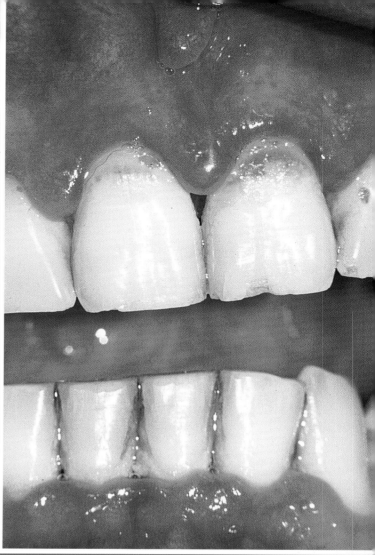

Plaque forms particularly where the teeth meet the gums and in the gaps between the teeth. The photo below shows a tooth with a cavity.

WHAT ARE BACTERIA?

Bacteria are the tiniest living things. Each bacterium is a single living **cell**, but they usually grow together in colonies of billions, often many different kinds together.

The cells in animals and plants have many different structures inside them, in particular a large **nucleus**. Bacterial cells however, are smaller and have no nucleus.

At birth your body contains no **bacteria**, but it begins to pick them up almost straight away. The saliva (spit) in the mouth contains **antibiotics** that kill some microbes. Those that are swallowed are killed by the strong **acid** in the stomach. But some microbes, mostly bacteria, survive and begin to grow.

Tooth microbes

Most of the microbes in the mouth live on the teeth. Large numbers of bacteria build up in these areas. They form a sticky coating called **plaque**, made up of bacteria, saliva and food particles.

Plaque is only a thin film on the teeth, but it contains millions of bacteria. The most common ones are two types of *Streptococcus*. Both of these produce acid as a waste product. The acid can cause tooth decay because it gradually wears away the hard **enamel** on the teeth. Regular brushing helps to stop the build-up of plaque and can prevent tooth decay.

Although too much plaque is a bad thing, it would not be good to remove all the microbes from the mouth. Harmless mouth microbes use up the space and food that might otherwise be taken up by disease-causing microbes. In fact, our normal mouth bacteria also produce chemicals that kill other bacteria. They do this for their own benefit, but it helps our body's defences too.

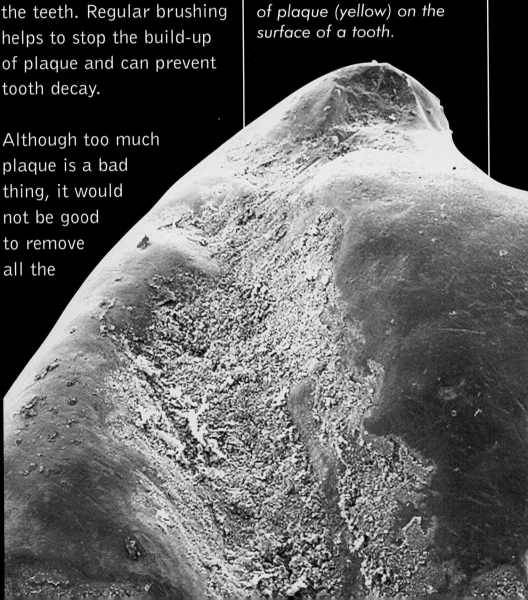

A *magnified (x200) photo of plaque (yellow) on the surface of a tooth.*

Bacteria in the gut

Microbes that are swallowed with food are killed by strong **acids** in the stomach. Because of this, the **small intestine**, where most **digestion** takes place, has very few microbes. But in the **large intestine** there are more **bacteria** than in any other part of the body.

The food that reaches the large intestine contains material that our bodies cannot use. But some bacteria can use our wastes as food, so they flourish in there.

The **gut** is like a long tube through the body. Food is mixed and digestion begins in the stomach (top, red). Most digestion takes place in the small intestine (blue), and wastes pass out through the large intestine or bowel (orange).

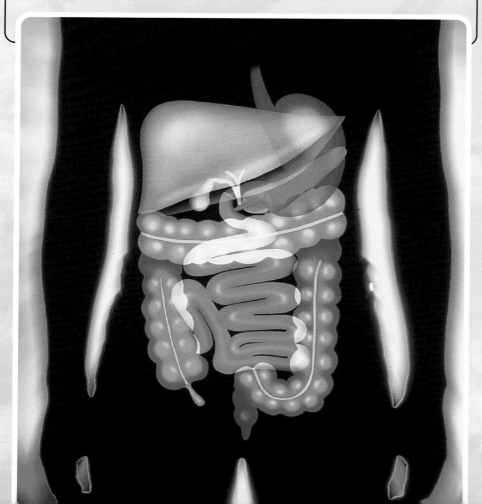

Chemical wizards

One of the main substances in plants is cellulose, a tough material that forms part of plant **cell** walls. Humans cannot break down cellulose, so it passes into the large intestine and out of the body. But many bacteria are chemical wizards, and can make use of foods that we cannot. There are bacteria that can break down cellulose, and many other human wastes.

Many of the bacteria in your large intestine are **anaerobic**. This means that they do not need to 'breathe'. When anaerobic microbes break down food for energy, the waste products are acids, alcohol or the gas, methane. If we have too many methane-

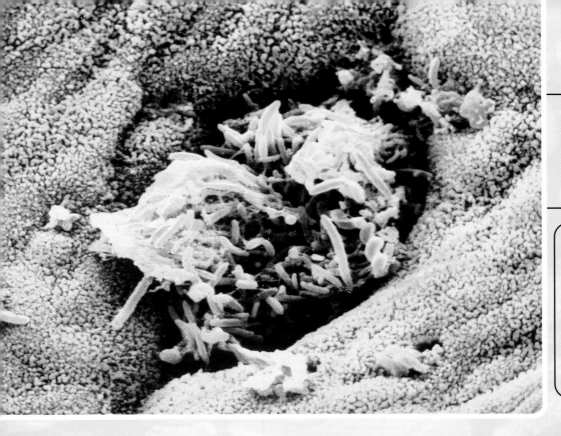

A *cluster of* Escherichia coli *bacteria settled on the wall of the large intestine (x4942).*

Bacteroides *(x19,585) is one of the anaerobic bacteria found in the large intestine.*

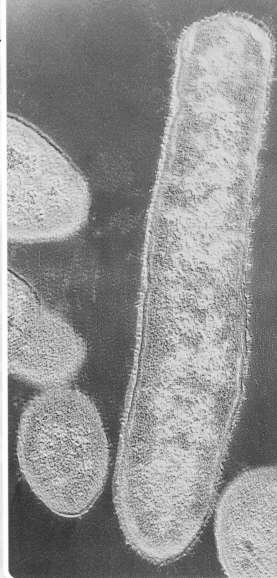

producing bacteria in our large intestine, this can cause 'gas' or **flatulence**.

Helpful bacteria

Like the bacteria in the mouth, those in the large intestine do us no harm. However, some gut bacteria are helpful. One group produce vitamin K, which is an important substance for making the blood **clot**. The bacteria make vitamin K for their own use, but when they die our body can absorb their vitamin K. Other bacteria in the gut produce B vitamins. This group of vitamins help us get energy from food, make sure our nerves work properly and are important for healthy skin, hair, eyes and liver.

OUTNUMBERED BY MICROBES

Our bodies are made up of billions of tiny cells but these cells are outnumbered by the bacteria in our large intestine. About 100,000 billion microbes live there – ten times the number of cells in our bodies. Many microbes are passed out of the body in the faeces (poo); bacteria make up 25–50% of the dry weight of faeces.

Trouble in the gut

Sometimes **bacteria** that don't belong there get into the **gut** and cause illness. They may cause food poisoning, **ulcers** and other diseases.

Food poisoning

Although stomach **acid** kills most bacteria, a few types are tough enough to survive. These bacteria get through the stomach because they are eaten with foods such as stale milk or meat, which reduce the strength of the stomach acid. One example is *Salmonella*, which causes food poisoning. Once they have got past the stomach, *Salmonella* bacteria invade the lining of the intestine. They produce toxins (poisons) that cause **diarrhoea** and vomiting (being sick).

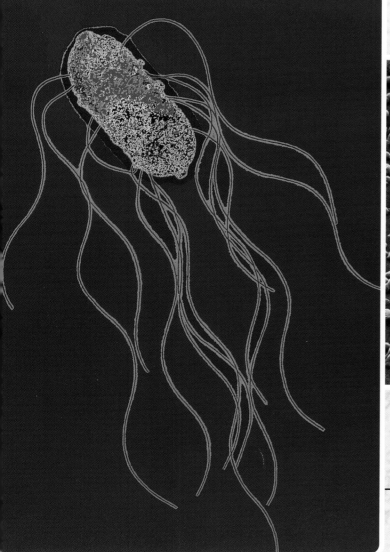

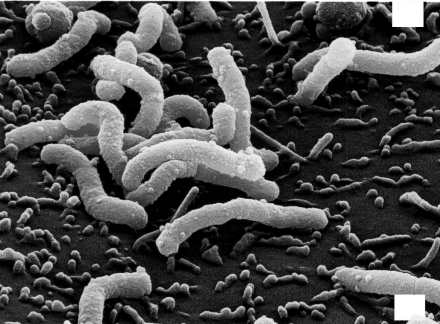

Helicobacter *bacteria on the surface of a human stomach cell.*

Salmonella *bacteria can grow in large numbers on food left out in warm conditions.*

Many other bacteria also cause food poisoning. Some, such as *Campylobacter*, are bacteria that normally live on the skin, but cause illness if large numbers get into the gut. With other bacteria, such as *Escherichia coli*, there are certain specific types that can cause disease.

Ulcers

Another kind of bacterium, called *Helicobacter*, doesn't just survive the stomach – it lives there! *Helicobacter* is a fragile, spiral bacterium ('helico' means spiral). So how does it survive in the harsh environment of the stomach?

The stomach lining has a thick coating of **mucus**, to protect the stomach walls from acid. *Helicobacter* survives by getting through this mucus coating and fastening itself to the stomach wall. The mucus that protects the stomach wall also protects the bacteria.

Many people have *Helicobacter* in their stomachs – more than half the people over 50 are infected. In some people it causes little harm. However, *Helicobacter* produces toxins which damage the stomach, and in some people this can cause stomach diseases such as ulcers and stomach cancer.

Microbes in the water

Cholera is a disease caused by a bacterium called *Vibrio cholerae*. It is rare in Europe and North America, but common in places such as India and parts of Africa. A person may get cholera by drinking **contaminated** water. The symptoms are diarrhoea, vomiting and leg cramps. Although cholera can be life-threatening, it is easily prevented and treated.

John Snow was a doctor in 19th-century London. He was the first doctor to recognize that cholera was transmitted by contaminated water.

Worms!

Do you have a dog or cat that has had worms? You might have had to go to the vet to get rid of them. People can get worms too, although they are much less common than in pets. **Tapeworms** and **hookworms** are just two of the many types of worm that are **parasites** of humans.

Tapeworms and hookworms are not related to each other, or to earthworms. Both live in the **gut**, but they get there by different routes and eat different foods.

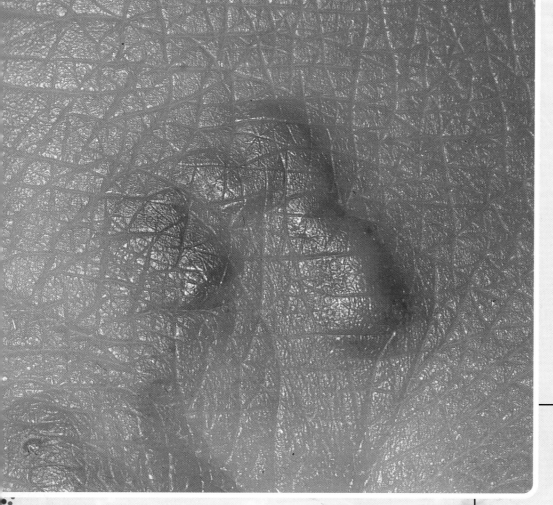

Hookworms

Hookworms are the kind of worms your dog or cat are most likely to get. Some types can infect humans, but this does not often happen in **developed countries** because they have better **sanitation** than in poorer countries.

Heavy infection with hookworm can create serious health problems for newborn babies, children, pregnant women and people who have a poor diet.

*If a hookworm **larva** gets into the body but cannot find a blood vessel, it causes a nasty rash.*

Getting into humans

Hookworm eggs begin life in the soil, where they hatch and grow into young worms. The young worms stand on their tails and wave their bodies in the air, 'questing' for a passing human. They most often get into the body by boring (making a hole) into the skin of someone walking barefoot. The tiny young hookworms wriggle into a blood vessel, and travel in the blood to the lungs, where they grow and develop further.

Becoming adults

When they are almost mature, the young hookworms are coughed out of the lungs and enter the **digestive** tract. They attach themselves to the wall of the **intestine**, where they live by sucking the **host**'s blood. Soon they start to lay eggs which pass out in the host's **faeces** (poo). In some countries, untreated **sewage** is deposited into rivers, and the river water is used for **irrigation**. If this happens, the eggs get into the soil, and the cycle begins again.

Effects of hookworms

When hookworms first get into the body, the place where they enter is itchy. Once they get into the gut, hookworms may make an adult feel a bit 'under the weather'. But children, and adults who are not eating well, can become very ill from hookworms. Drugs will get rid of hookworms, but it is important to improve the diet to become completely healthy again.

A hookworm (x495) uses its 'teeth' to cling to its host's intestines.

Tapeworms

Hookworms are only about a centimetre long. **Tapeworms** are a few millimetres wide, but they can be 10 metres long! These giant **parasites** only live in humans as adults – their young live in another **host** animal. The pork tapeworm, for instance, spends its early life inside a pig.

Magnified view (x74) of the scolex of a pork tapeworm, showing the ring of hooks and suckers.

Adult tapeworms live in human **intestines**, but unlike hookworms, they eat by absorbing **digested** food from the intestine. People most commonly get tapeworms by eating

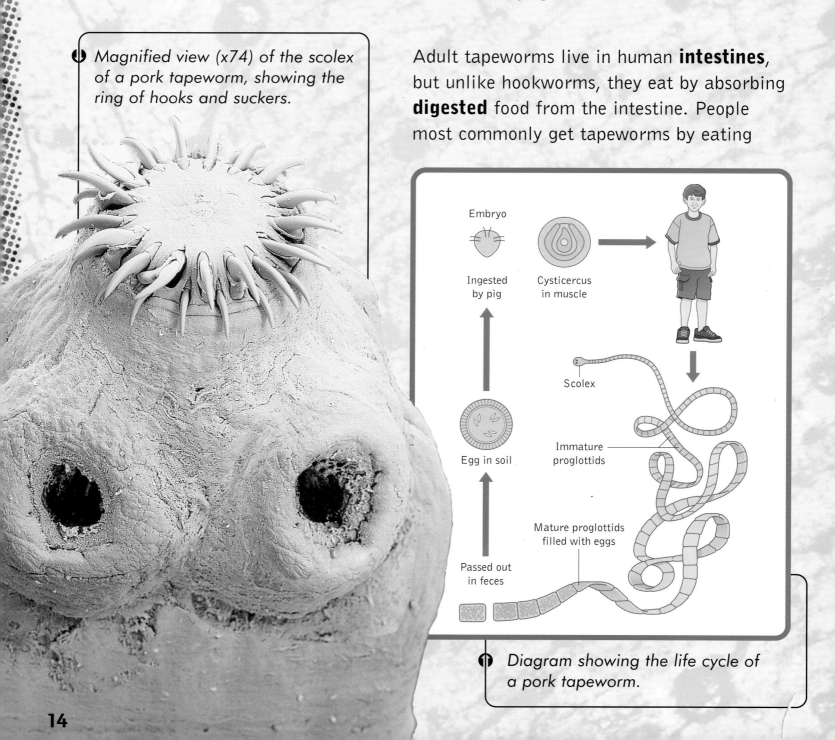

Embryo

Ingested by pig

Cysticercus in muscle

Scolex

Egg in soil

Immature proglottids

Mature proglottids filled with eggs

Passed out in feces

Diagram showing the life cycle of a pork tapeworm.

contaminated food that has not been cooked properly (when food is heated through during cooking any microbes in it are killed off). However, food safety laws have virtually got rid of tapeworms in **developed countries**.

The pork tapeworm

The pork tapeworm fastens to the wall of the human host's intestines using a ring of hooks and suckers on its head, which is called a **scolex**. It then grows a long string of segments (up to 4000 of them), each one containing thousands of eggs. When a segment is mature, it drops off the end of the worm, and passes out in the host's **faeces** (poo). A large tapeworm can shed up to a million eggs a day.

Tapeworm eggs hatch into **larvae**. The larvae need to be eaten by a pig to develop further. This can happen if, for instance, pigs are fed plants that have been **irrigated** with water

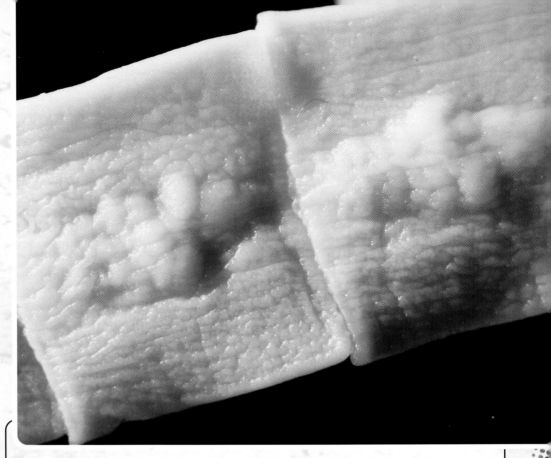

The fish tapeworm is the longest kind found in humans. It can live for 20 years. Here you can see a close-up of the tapeworm sections bulging with developing eggs.

contaminated by untreated human sewage. Once the larvae have been eaten, they get into the pig's blood and travel to the muscles. Here each one forms a tough ball called a **cyst**.

If the pig is killed for meat, the cysts get into another human. Once it reaches the human intestine the cyst splits and turns itself inside out to become the head of a new adult tapeworm. The cycle is ready to begin again.

Tapeworm symptoms

As with hookworms, a healthy adult can be infected with a tapeworm and have only vague discomfort for a time. However, a bad tapeworm infection can cause **diarrhoea** and vomiting. Some people are constantly hungry because the tapeworms are eating most of their food. Drugs can get rid of the worm.

Microbes in the nose and throat

When you breathe in, tiny particles of dust get into your nose and throat along with the air. Some of this 'dust' is **microbes** such as **bacteria** and **viruses**. Scientists estimate that we inhale 10,000 new microbes every day.

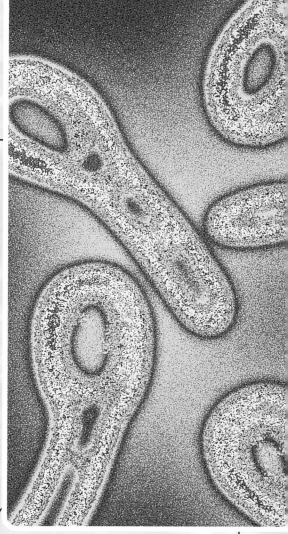

Corynebacterium *can be club-shaped, as here (x100,000). Some kinds can cause the serious disease, diptheria.*

Staphylococcus *bacteria (round yellow shapes) on the lining of the nose (x17,160). The nose is lined with tiny hairs called cilia. The bacteria cling to the* **mucus** *(blue) on the cilia.*

Many of the microbes that we inhale are trapped and killed by the body's defences. However, some survive and live in the nose and throat.

Bacteria

Two main groups of bacteria live in the nose and throat. One group are small, round

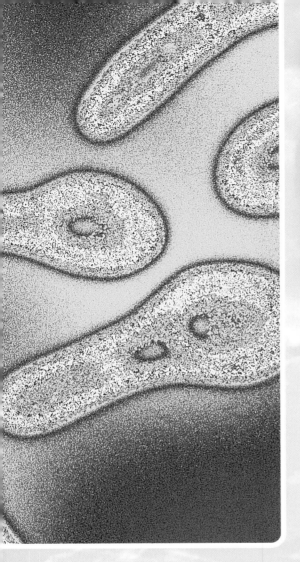

VIRUSES

Viruses are tiny particles made of an outer layer made mainly of **protein**, and an inner core of **DNA**.

Outside of another living cell, a virus cannot move, eat, grow or reproduce. Viruses infect cells by injecting their DNA into the cell. Then the virus takes control — it puts the cell's machinery to work making copies of the virus. Eventually the cell becomes overloaded and bursts, releasing thousands of viruses to infect other cells.

Corynebacterium. These bacteria are sausage-shaped rather than round.

Smaller than bacteria

Also living in the nose and throat are even smaller microbes called viruses. Some viruses live in the nose and throat even in healthy people. Viruses differ from other creatures because they can only grow and reproduce when they are inside the **cells** of another living thing (see box).

There are all kinds of different viruses in the nose and throat. Adenoviruses live mainly on the tonsils, while myxoviruses live in the tissues of the nose and throat. Rhinoviruses are

Adenoviruses are not round. They look like crystals, with 20 flat, triangular-shaped faces (x167,650).

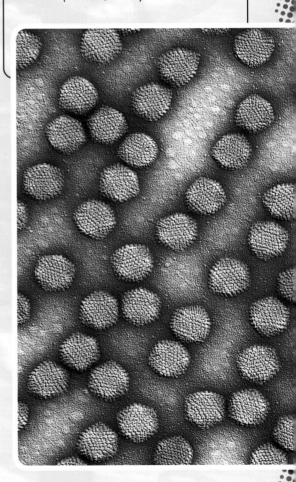

bacteria called *Staphylococcus* (a coccus is any kind of round or oval-shaped bacterium). They grow in chains, or in clusters, like bunches of grapes. Some kinds of *Staphylococcus* can cause illness, but others live in the nose and throat without causing any harm.

The other bacteria common in the nose and throat lining are a group called

extremely tiny viruses that also live in the nose and throat.

Sore throats, colds and flu

Aaaaa-choo! Sneezes, coughing and a runny nose usually mean a cold or flu. Colds and flu are caused when the **viruses** in your nose and throat get past the defences that normally keep them in check. **Bacteria** can also cause illnesses such as sore throats.

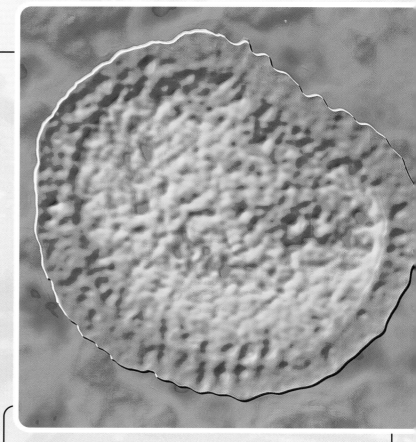

The hair-like cilia (pink) that line the throat clear out most of the microbes before they can take hold (x1970).

This is the influenza virus (x462,185), which causes flu. Other viruses in the nose cause different illness.

Getting a cold

Colds are caused by very tiny viruses known as rhinoviruses. There are many different kinds of rhinovirus, and each kind can sometimes **mutate** (change), which fools your body's defences.

If a rhinovirus manages to get into one of the **cells** that line the nose, it takes over and makes copies of itself. Eventually the cell bursts open and releases lots of new viruses, which invade more cells.

Although cold viruses damage the nose lining, they don't cause cold symptoms. These are mainly due to the body's response to the infection. The body releases chemicals that increase the flow of **mucus** in the nose, and cause sneezing and coughing. The combination of sneezing, coughing and a runny nose help to clear viruses out of the nose and throat.

Bacterial infections

Bacteria can also cause sore throats or tonsillitis

TONSILLITIS

The tonsils are two pink balls in the back of the throat. You can see them if you stand in front of a mirror, open your mouth, stick out your tongue and say, 'Aaahh'.

The job of the tonsils is to catch incoming microbes and stop them from causing infections. Sometimes the tonsils themselves get infected, and the result is tonsillitis. Usually gargling, painkillers and keeping the throat cool will get rid of the infection, but sometimes antibiotics are needed and occasionally people have to have their tonsils removed.

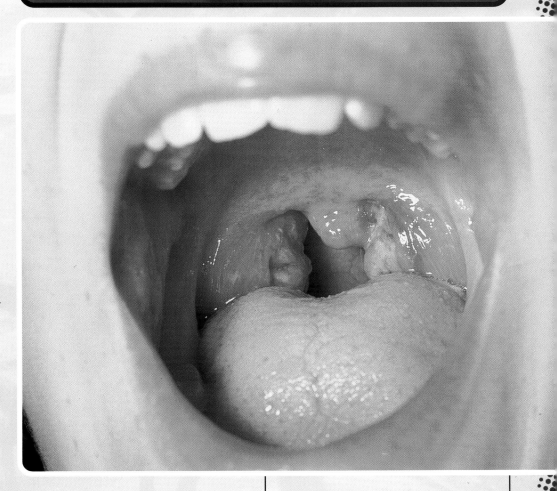

Tonsils swollen by infection with Streptococcus *bacteria*.

(see box). A bacterium that causes sore throats is called *Streptococcus*, so this kind of sore throat is called 'strep throat'. A strep throat can feel very sore, but doctors can treat it with **antibiotics** (drugs that kill bacteria). However, these drugs do not work for viral sore throats.

Microbes in the lungs

When a healthy person breathes, **microbes** don't get any further into the body than the throat. But sometimes microbes do get into the lungs, and cause diseases.

Any microbes that get beyond the throat are usually trapped in a thick layer of **mucus** that covers the walls of the tubes. They are then pushed out of the lungs by millions of tiny hairs called **cilia**, which waft the microbes up into the throat. The microbes are then swallowed, and killed by the **acids** in the stomach.

Getting into the lungs

Some microbes can, however, get past this first line of defence. They have special chemicals on the outside that allow them to fasten on to the lung lining. Then other chemicals called **invasins** help them get into the body.

Pneumonia

One disease caused by lung infection is pneumonia. Pneumonia is a serious infection in which some of the air sacs in the lungs become inflamed (swell up). This

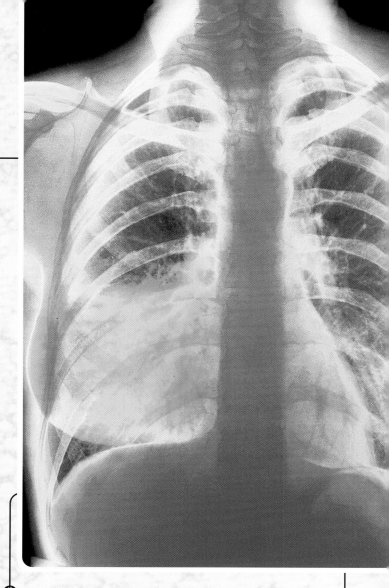

X-ray of the lungs of someone with pneumonia. In the affected area (light blue) the air sacs get blocked with pus causing the lung to solidify.

causes breathlessness, a chesty cough, fever, chills and chest pain.

Pneumonia can have several different causes. One type is caused by *Streptococcus* **bacteria**, similar to the ones that cause strep throat. Several different **viruses** can also cause other types of pneumonia, although they are not as serious.

Another mild type of pneumonia is caused by **mycoplasmas**, which are very, very small, unusual bacteria. All other bacteria have a tough outer wall, but mycoplasmas have only a thin, flexible membrane (skin).

Whooping cough and TB

Two other lung diseases are whooping cough and tuberculosis (TB). Both are spread by the coughs and sneezes of infected people, which spray tiny droplets containing the bacteria into the air.

A bacterium called *Bordetella* causes whooping cough. In the past it was a serious disease, but now there is a **vaccine** against it.

TB is caused by the bacterium *Mycobacterium tuberculosis*. It usually starts as a lung disease, but it can spread to other parts of the body. The disease causes fever, weight loss, and constant coughing. Drugs have been developed against TB, but the disease is still a problem in poor countries, where there is not enough money for good health care and drugs.

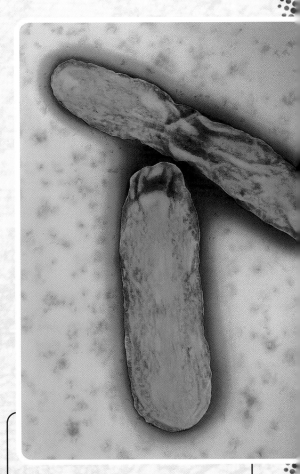

Mycobacterium tuberculosis, *the bacterium that causes tuberculosis (x25,035).*

Babies in many countries are given a single vaccination that protects them against three diseases – whooping cough, diphtheria and tetanus.

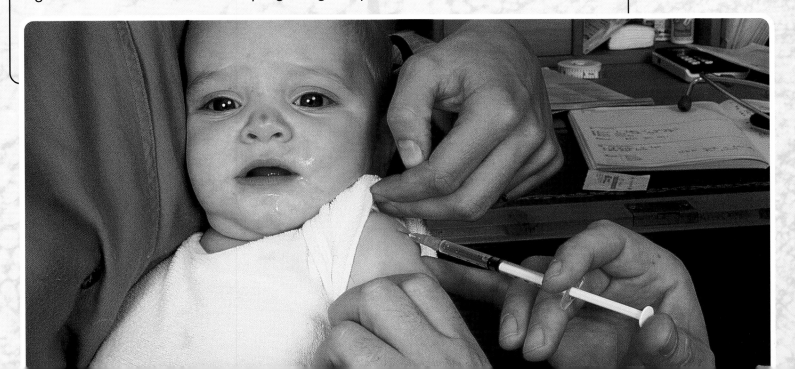

Microbes in the blood

Your skin seems quite thin and not very tough, but it is an effective barrier against all kinds of **microbes**. However, sometimes the skin is broken by a cut or a scrape.

Wound defences

If you get a cut or a scrape, the body's defence systems go into action. The blood at the site of the wound **clots** (goes hard), and the clot becomes a barrier to microbes. Also lots of **white blood cells** rush to the site of the wound. Some of these blood cells can 'eat' microbes. Other white blood cells break open and release chemicals that kill microbes.

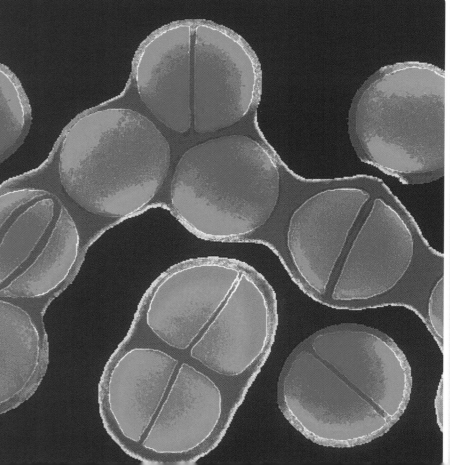

Ouch! If you get a cut or a scrape, it hurts! The pain is an alarm signal to your body's defence system.

Staphylococcus *bacteria like these (x26,890) can cause infection of a cut.*

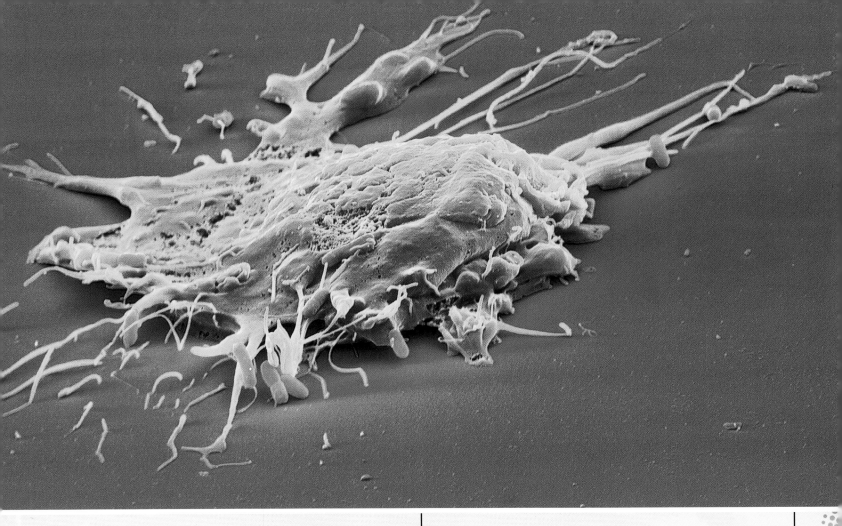

Septic cuts

If you clean a wound carefully and then cover it with a bandage or a plaster, the body can usually heal itself. However, a deep wound (for instance from a nail) might be difficult to clean, and may get infected. If this happens, the area around the cut may get red and begin to swell, as more and more white blood cells arrive to combat the infection. The wound may also produce a yellow discharge called pus, which is made up of dead microbes and the remains of white blood cells.

If **bacteria** or other microbes get out of the local area of the wound and into the blood, they can travel in the bloodstream and cause infection elsewhere.

A white blood cell reaching out long 'feelers' to engulf several bacteria (pink, rod-shaped) (x5882). Once inside the blood cell, the bacteria are broken down.

Infection microbes

The microbes that usually get into a wound are ones that are normally found on the skin, such as some kinds of *Staphylococcus*. However, sometimes bacteria from soil or other places get into a wound and cause illness. Tetanus, for instance, is a disease in which the muscles go into **spasm**. It is caused by a bacterium normally found in the soil. Tetanus used to be a serious danger, but in many countries people are now **vaccinated** against the disease.

Diseases from bloodsuckers

Sometimes **microbes** get past the body's outer defences by being injected directly into the blood. This can happen if you get bitten by a bloodsucking insect or other animal. Mosquitoes, ticks and fleas are three bloodsuckers that can pass on disease this way.

All of us have been bitten by mosquitoes, midges, or other bloodsuckers. Most of the time the bite causes nothing more than an itchy lump. But occasionally the insect that bites you is carrying microbes that cause disease, and these get injected into your blood.

A mosquito feeding on a human. Only female mosquitoes are bloodsuckers: male mosquitoes drink nectar from flowers.

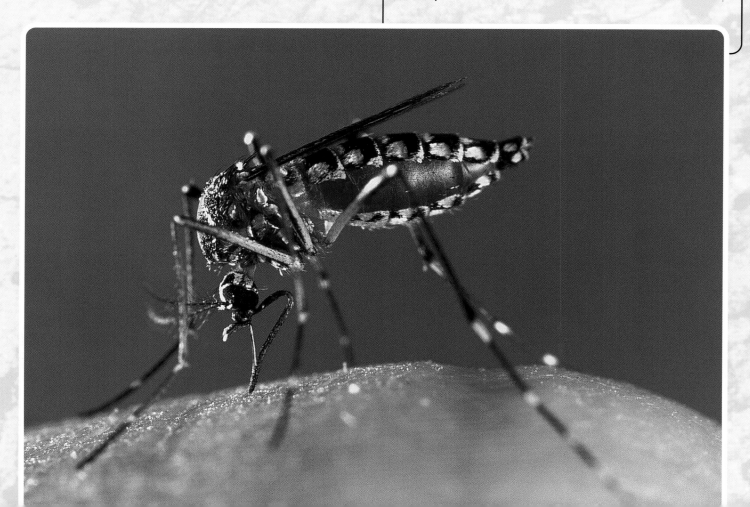

Insect-carried diseases are a particular problem in hot tropical countries.

When a bloodsucker bites a person, it injects saliva (spit) into the wound. Chemicals in the saliva stop the blood from **clotting**. If the bloodsucker is carrying a disease, microbes get into the blood with the saliva.

Mosquitoes

Mosquitoes are carriers of more diseases than any other bloodsuckers. They can carry malaria, a disease which causes lots of human deaths every year (see page 26). They can also carry other diseases. The West Nile virus is carried by mosquitoes and causes a flu-like fever, but it can have more severe effects such as swelling of the brain (encephalitis).

Ticks

Ticks are eight-legged bloodsuckers that are relations of spiders. One illness that can be passed on in tick bites is Lyme disease. It is caused by a spiral-shaped **bacteria**

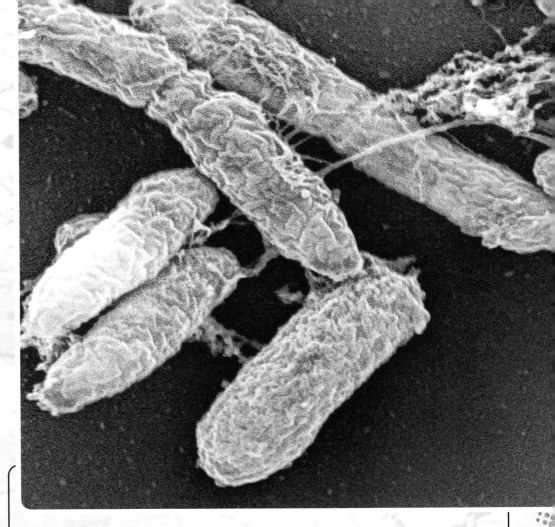

❶ The bacteria that cause plague, Yersinia pestis.

called *Borrelia*. Lyme disease starts with a rash around the site of the tick bite, but then causes arthritis (painful swelling of joints).

Fleas

The fleas that sometimes infest our pets and occasionally bite us are not often disease carriers. But they can pass on **tapeworms** to dogs and cats if they accidentally swallow them (see page 14).

In fact, several other diseases can be carried by fleas.

The bacteria that cause plague, *Yersinia*, are carried by rat fleas. Plague is a disease that we think of as belonging to the past, but there are still regular outbreaks in Africa, Asia and South America. Plague makes people feverish and exhausted, and they get painful swellings in their armpits and necks.

Protozoans

Bacteria and **viruses** are not the only **microbes** that live inside us. Larger single-celled creatures called **protozoans** also live there. Some are **parasites** and cause disease, but others are **predators** that feed on other microbes.

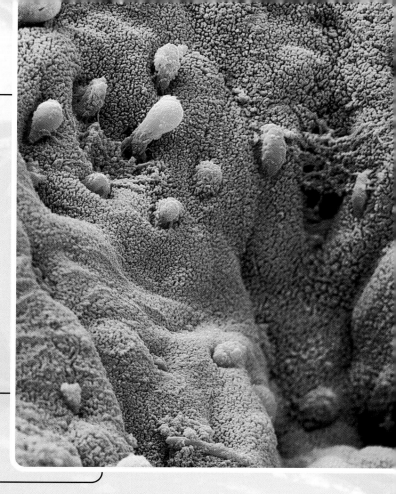

Amoebas (blue) attached to and feeding on the lining of the large intestine (x3177).

Magnified view (x2550) of the blood of someone with sleeping sickness, showing the Trypansoma *flagellates* that cause the disease (blue) amongst the red blood cells (grey, round).

Amoebas

Amoebas are a kind of protozoan that live in the mouth and other parts of the **gut**. They get into the mouth on food or from our fingers, and feed on bacteria and small food particles.

An amoeba is a jelly-like blob with a thin, flexible membrane ('skin'). It moves by sending out long 'fingers' called **pseudopods**, which attach to the surface then pull the amoeba forward. Amoebas

also use their pseudopods to catch food. One kind of amoeba that can get into the gut feeds on the wall of the stomach or **intestines** instead of feeding on bacteria. This kind of amoeba can cause bad **diarrhoea**.

Other protozoans

Other kinds of protozoans can also get into the gut and cause disease. A tiny, slipper-shaped protozoan called *Giardia* belongs to a group of protozoans called **flagellates**. It can infect

the **small intestine** if people eat food or drink water that has been **contaminated** by **sewage**. *Giardia* infections often cause diarrhoea.

Other flagellates live in the blood and are spread by bloodsucking insects. One kind causes sleeping sickness, a serious disease in tropical Africa that is spread by a fly.

Malaria

Malaria is one of the most serious diseases in humans. In the hot regions of Africa, southern Asia and South America millions of people get the disease each year,

and many of them die. Malaria is caused by a protozoan called *Plasmodium*. It begins its life in a mosquito, and gets into a person's blood when the mosquito takes a meal. The protozoans mostly infect red blood cells. They multiply until the blood cell bursts, and then they look for another cell to invade. If another mosquito feeds on a person infected with malaria it might pick up protozoans from their blood, and the disease cycle starts again.

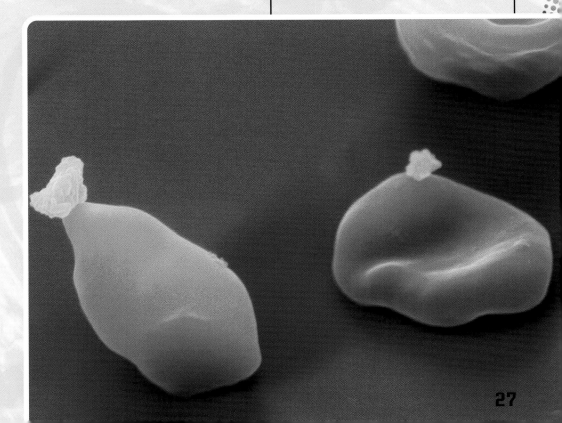

Plasmodium *protozoans (yellow) emerging from red blood cells (x10,040).*

Table of sizes

Although all hidden life is tiny, there is a huge range of sizes. To a flea, a grain of pollen seems just as tiny as the flea seems to us!

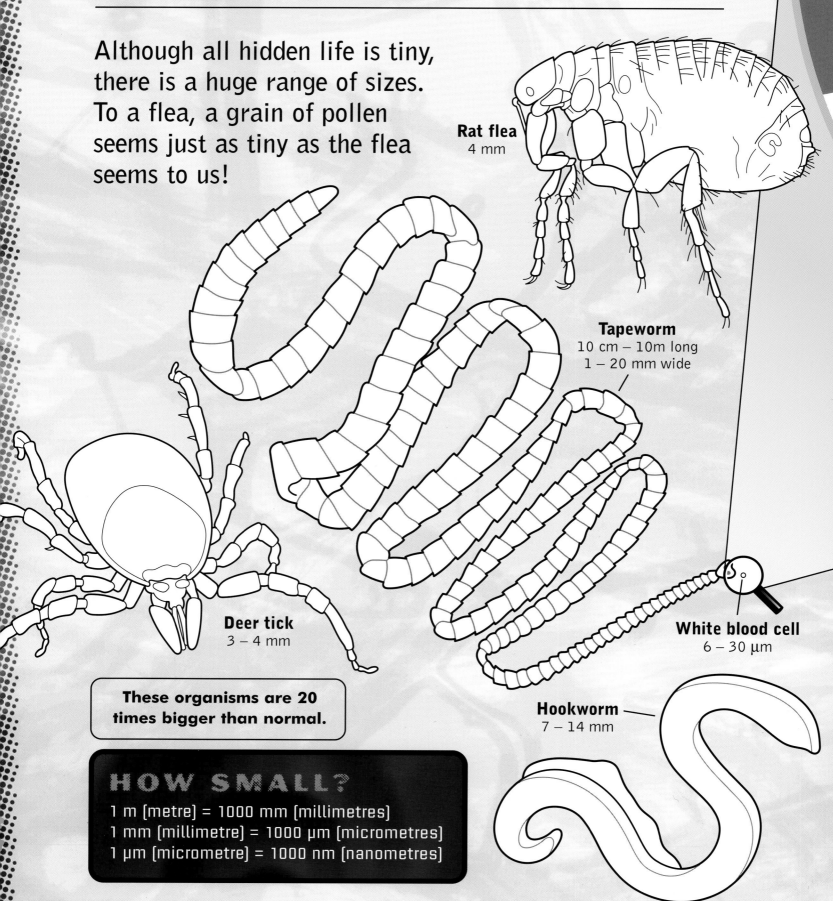

Rat flea
4 mm

Tapeworm
10 cm – 10m long
1 – 20 mm wide

Deer tick
3 – 4 mm

White blood cell
6 – 30 µm

Hookworm
7 – 14 mm

These organisms are 20 times bigger than normal.

HOW SMALL?

1 m [metre] = 1000 mm [millimetres]
1 mm [millimetre] = 1000 µm [micrometres]
1 µm [micrometre] = 1000 nm [nanometres]

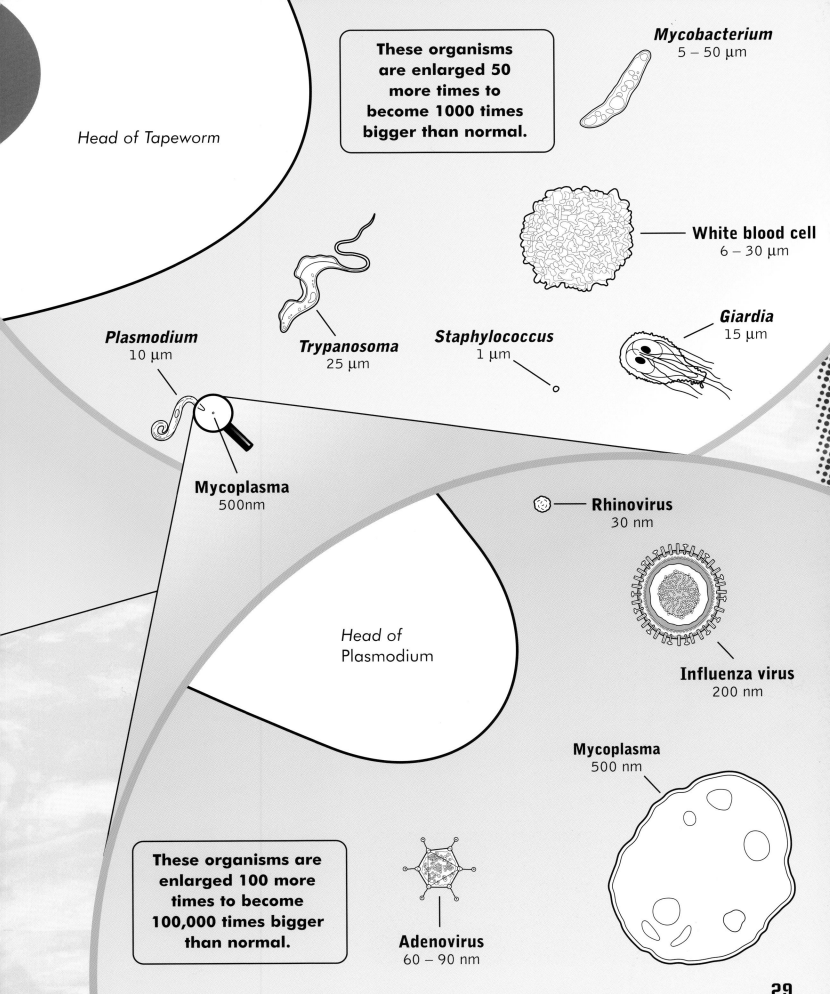

Head of Tapeworm

These organisms are enlarged 50 more times to become 1000 times bigger than normal.

Mycobacterium
5 – 50 μm

White blood cell
6 – 30 μm

Plasmodium
10 μm

Trypanosoma
25 μm

Staphylococcus
1 μm

Giardia
15 μm

Mycoplasma
500nm

Head of Plasmodium

Rhinovirus
30 nm

Influenza virus
200 nm

Mycoplasma
500 nm

These organisms are enlarged 100 more times to become 100,000 times bigger than normal.

Adenovirus
60 – 90 nm

Glossary

acid   sour, sharp or corrosive substance. Lemons and vinegar are acidic.

anaerobic   without air. Anaerobic microbes can live without air.

antibiotics   drugs that kill bacteria or stop them growing

bacteria   (singular – bacterium) very tiny creatures, each one only a single cell. They are different from other single-celled creatures because they don't have a nucleus.

cells   the building blocks of living things. Some living things are just single cells, others are made up of billions of cells working together.

cilia   (singular – cilium) tiny 'hairs' that stick out from the surface of some microbes. They can move in a co-ordinated way to propel the microbe along or waft food towards it.

clot   lump of hardened blood

contaminated   when food or something else becomes dirty or infected with disease microbes

cyst   round capsule with a tough outer coat. Pork hookworms form cysts in the muscles of pigs.

developed countries   rich countries such as those of Europe and North America, where most people work in offices and factories rather than as farmers

diarrhoea   watery faeces

digestion   breaking down of the food we eat into nutrients that the body can absorb and use for energy

DNA   material that makes up the genes of living cells

electron microscopes   very powerful microscopes that can magnify objects up to half a million times

enamel   hard protective coating on the outside of teeth

faeces   waste from your digestive system: poo

flagellates   group of protozoans that have one or more long, whip-like flagella (hairs)

flatulence   trapped air in the gut causing discomfort and farting

gut   digestive tract, which includes the stomach and intestines

hookworms   small roundworms that are parasites of humans and other animals

host   animal or plant that a parasite lives on

intestines   small intestine and large intestine

invasins   chemicals produced by disease microbes that help them to invade the body

irrigation   to water fields of crops

large intestine   the last part of the gut, where water is absorbed from waste food and the waste becomes faeces (poo)

larvae   (singular – larva) the young stage of some types of creatures. Larvae look different from adults, and may have to go through a changing stage in order to become adults.

metabolism   all the chemical activity that goes on inside a living cell, or collection of cells

microbes   microscopic creatures such as bacteria, protozoa, fungi and viruses

mucus   thick, gooey liquid that helps to protect the lining of the air tubes and the gut

mutate   to change identifying features

mycoplasmas   very small bacteria that do not have a hard outer cell wall

nucleus   round structure surrounded by a membrane, found inside a living cell. It contains the cell's genes.

nutrients   chemicals that nourish living things

parasites   creatures that live on or in another living creature and take their food from it, without giving any benefit in return

plaque   thin film of bacteria that covers parts of the teeth

predators   animals that hunt and kill other animals for food

proteins   substances that are used to build structures within living things and to control the thousands of chemical reactions that happen inside cells

protozoans   single-celled creatures that have a larger, more complicated cell structure than bacteria

pseudopods   finger-like projections that amoebas use to move themselves about or to capture food

sanitation   keeping houses and streets clean, making sure that food is safe to eat and disposing of waste safely

scolex   head of a tapeworm, including a circle of hooks and suckers, which it uses to attach to the intestines

sewage   waste from sinks, bathrooms and toilets

small intestine   main part of the gut, a long tube between the stomach and the large intestine where the body absorbs most of the nutrients from our food

spasms sudden, uncontrollable contractions (shortening) of the muscles

tapeworms long flatworms made up of many segments that are parasites of humans and other animals

ulcers sores on the lining of the stomach or intestines

vaccine a substance that protects someone from getting a particular disease by stimulating the body's defences against that disease

virus an extremely tiny microbe that cannot grow or reproduce by itself, but has to infect a living cell to do so

white blood cells cells in the blood that play an important part in defending the body against disease

further reading

Cells and Life: The Diversity of Life, Robert Snedden, (Heinemann Library, 2002)

Cells and Life: The World of the Cell, Robert Snedden, (Heinemann Library, 2002)

DK Mega Bites: Microlife: The Microscopic World of Tiny Creatures, David Burnie, (Dorling Kindersley, 2002)

Microlife: A World of Microorganisms, Robert Snedden, (Heinemann Library, 2000)

Websites

Cells Alive! (www.cellsalive.com)
Pictures, videos and interactive pages about cells and microbes. The How Big? page shows the sizes of creatures from mites to viruses.

Virtual Microscopy (www.micro.magnet.fsu.edu/primer/virtual/virtual.html)
On this interactive website you can pick from a selection of samples, adjust the focus, change the magnification, and use a whole range of powerful microscopes.

Microbe Zoo (www.commtechlab.msu.edu/sites/dlc-me/zoo/)
A site about strange microbes.

Microbe World (www.microbeworld.org/home.htm)
Information, pictures, movies and activities exploring the world of microbes.

Index

Titles in the *Hidden Life* series include:

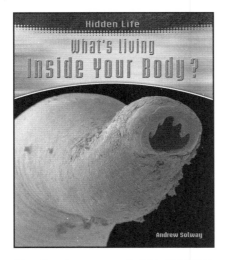

Hardback   0 431 18962 5

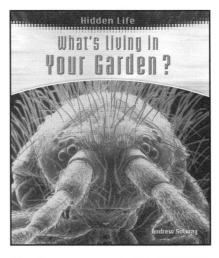

Hardback   0 431 18965 X

Hardback   0 431 18964 1

Hardback   0 431 18963 3

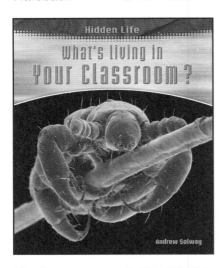

Hardback   0 431 18966 8

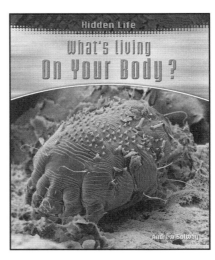

Hardback   0 431 18961 7

Find out about the other titles in this series on our website www.heinemann.co.uk/library